Love Journal

Love Journal

SWEET STORIES, SHARED REFLECTIONS, AND KEEPSAKES

Laura Buller

Bluestreak
BOOKS

Bluestreak

Weldon Owen International
1150 Brickyard Cove Rd. First Floor, Richmond, CA 94801
www.weldonowen.com

Edited by Madeleine Calvi and designed by Megan Sinead Harris.

Library of Congress Cataloging in Publication data is available.

ISBN: 978-1-68188-506-3

First Printed in 2020
10 9 8 7 6 5 4 3 2 1
2019 2020 2021 2022

Printed and bound in China.

This one goes out to the one I love

How to use this book:

Throughout this journal, you'll find prompts that will help you explore your relationship as a couple, as well as your past, your present, and your future together. You and your partner in love will each complete your own profiles at the start of the book, with one of you choosing the I AM section and the other filling out the YOU ARE section. Throughout the pages you'll each answer different prompts. You may want to brainstorm together to fill in the journal. You can also complete your love story by passing the book back and forth or interviewing each other. The goal is for you to share and communicate with each other, and to record your thoughts, feelings, memories, and dreams together.

Some pages ask you to add your own photos or keepsakes (ticket stubs, menus, love notes, cards, or letters) using photo corners or other scrapbooking supplies. If you don't have a photo, you can get creative and use more words or sketch a picture of the moment. At the back of the book, you'll find an envelope where you can keep more photos and keepsake memories that tell your love story, and preserve them for years to come. Your story is unique; use this journal to capture it and share your love.

Contents

INTRODUCTION

"To me, you are perfect."
— *Love Actually*

Love is all around us. Just think about all the songs, books, and movies that tell a myriad of love stories. We can't help falling in love: first glances to lingering looks, secrets shared and memories made, being true to ourselves while building trust in each other. Even though countless love stories have already been told, there is one that is absolutely special: your own. With this journal, you will be encouraged to capture your own sweet story, explore the ways you found love together, share your secret thoughts, and record your hopes and dreams for a love that is forever after.

PART ONE

You and Me

I AM...

Whoever has chosen I AM, fill in the corresponding prompts throughout the rest of this book.

My full name is _____

But you call me _____

_____

I was born on _____

I am older than / younger than / same age as you (*Circle one*)

Meet my family: _____

_____

_____

_____

_____

_____

_____

I grew up in _____

_____

_____

Here's a picture or keepsake from before we met:

YOU ARE...

Whoever has chosen YOU ARE, fill in the corresponding prompts throughout the rest of this book.

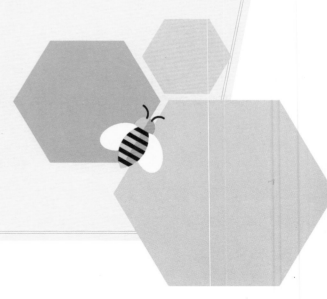

My full name is _____

But you call me _____

_____

I was born on _____

I am older than / younger than / same age as you (*Circle one*)

Meet my family: _____

_____

_____

_____

_____

I grew up in _____

_____

_____

Here's a picture or keepsake from before we met:

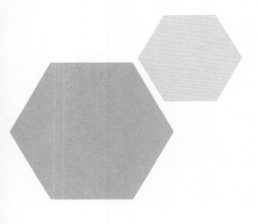

ME BEFORE YOU

Describe your childhood home.

My hometown was _____

_____

The best part of being a kid was _____

_____

_____

_____

Some of my favorite things were _____

_____

_____

What hasn't changed about me? _____

_____

_____

If you knew me back then, you might have:

☐ Pulled my hair

☐ Chased me around the monkey bars

☐ Ignored me

☐ Other: _____

_____

Add a photo of yourself as a child:

YOU BEFORE ME

Describe your childhood home.

My hometown was _____

_____

The best part of being a kid was _____

_____

_____

_____

Some of my favorite things were _____

_____

_____

_____

What hasn't changed about me? _____

_____

_____

_____

If you knew me back then, you might have:

☐ Pulled my hair

☐ Chased me around the monkey bars

☐ Ignored me

☐ Other: _____

_____

_____

Add a photo of yourself as a child:

HELLO? IS IT ME YOU'RE LOOKING FOR?

What was happening in my life just before we met? _____

_____

_____

_____

Where was I living and what did I do? _____

_____

_____

_____

What was I looking for, and what were my dreams? _____

_____

_____

_____

_____

Who did I confide in? _____

_____

Is there a funny story about my dreams not exactly coming true? _____

_____

_____

_____

_____

_____

Here's a photo or memento from the time just before we met:

HELLO? IS IT YOU I'M LOOKING FOR?

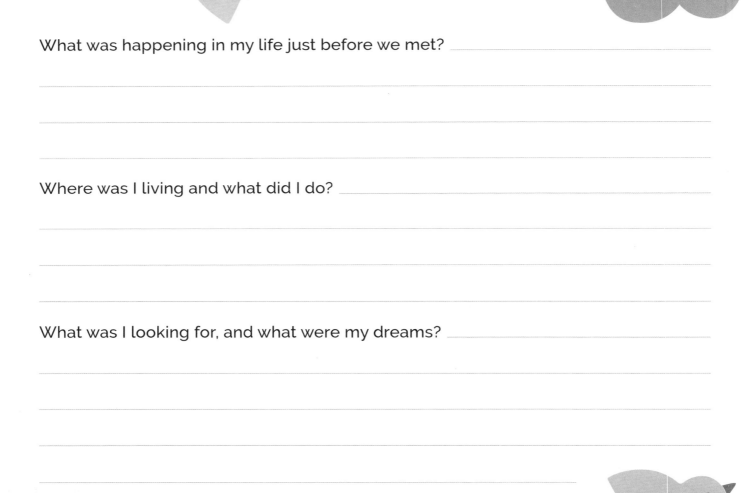

What was happening in my life just before we met? _____

_____

_____

Where was I living and what did I do? _____

_____

_____

What was I looking for, and what were my dreams? _____

_____

_____

_____

Who did I confide in? _____

_____

_____

Is there a funny story about my dreams not exactly coming true? _____

_____

_____

_____

_____

Here's a photo or memento from the time just before we met:

PART TWO

Our Love Story

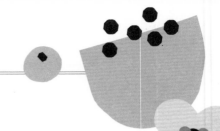

THE FIRST TIME EVER I

Set the scene for your first meeting.

Here's one word to describe the moment we met: _____

Here's what I noticed about you: _____

_____

_____

_____

PS: I was secretly thinking _____

_____

_____

_____

_____

_____

_____

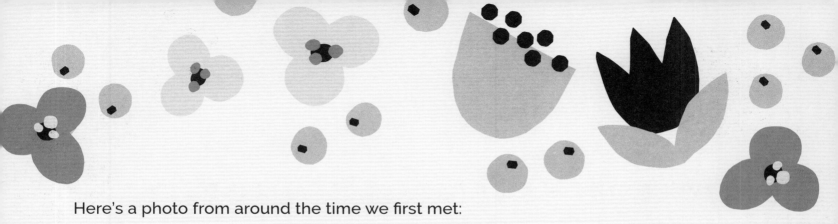

Here's a photo from around the time we first met:

"Where there is love there is life."

— *Mahatma Gandhi*

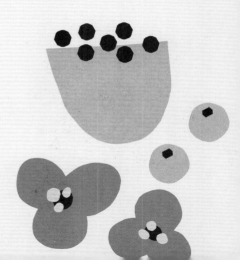

THE FIRST TIME YOU EVER

Set the scene for your first meeting.

Here's one word to describe the moment we met: _____

_____

Here's what I noticed about you: _____

_____

_____

_____

PS: I was secretly thinking _____

_____

_____

_____

_____

_____

Here's a photo from around the time we first met:

"We are most alive when we're in love."

— *John Updike*

MY RESPONSES:

What were you wearing? _____

_____

_____

If we talked, what did we say? _____

_____

_____

_____

Did anything funny or unusual happen? _____

_____

_____

_____

Did we plan to meet again? _____

_____

_____

_____

Be honest! Yes, no, or maybe: Love at first sight? _____

_____

_____

_____

YOUR RESPONSES:

What were you wearing? _____

_____

_____

If we talked, what did we say? _____

_____

_____

Did anything funny or unusual happen? _____

_____

_____

_____

Did we plan to meet again? _____

_____

_____

Be honest! Yes, no, or maybe: Love at first sight? _____

_____

_____

SPARKS FLY

When I thought about you, what made my heart beat a little faster?

MY RESPONSE: _____

_____

_____

_____

YOUR RESPONSE: _____

_____

_____

What did I tell my friends and family about you?

MY RESPONSE: _____

_____

_____

YOUR RESPONSE: _____

_____

I couldn't stop thinking about:

MY RESPONSE: _____

_____

_____

YOUR RESPONSE: _____

_____

_____

_____

But I might not have been so sure about:

MY RESPONSE: _____

_____

_____

YOUR RESPONSE: _____

_____

_____

FIRST DATE

Set the scene for your first date.

Where did we go and what did we do?

MY RESPONSE: _____

_____

_____

YOUR RESPONSE: _____

_____

_____

Were there any silly moments?

MY RESPONSE: _____

_____

_____

YOUR RESPONSE: _____

_____

What made it memorable for me?

MY RESPONSE: _____

_____

_____

YOUR RESPONSE: _____

_____

_____

_____

Describe any mementos you may have kept:

MY RESPONSE: _____

_____

_____

YOUR RESPONSE: _____

_____

_____

"Love makes your soul crawl out
from its hiding place."

— *Zora Neale Hurston*

A KISS

When and where did we share our first kiss? _____

MY RESPONSE: _____

_____

_____

YOUR RESPONSE: _____

_____

_____

Choose one and explain why:

MY RESPONSE:

☐ Explosive fireworks

☐ A bright sparkler

☐ An unlit match

☐ Other

Because _____

_____

_____

_____

_____

YOUR RESPONSE:

☐ Explosive fireworks

☐ A bright sparkler

☐ An unlit match

☐ Other

Because _____

_____

_____

_____

Your kiss made me feel:

MY RESPONSE: _____

_____

_____

YOUR RESPONSE: _____

_____

_____

How long before it happened again?

MY RESPONSE: _____

_____

YOUR RESPONSE: _____

_____

"Love has nothing to do with what you are expecting to get—only what you are expecting to give— which is everything."

— *Katharine Hepburn*

KNOWING ME,
KNOWING YOU

As we got to know each other, how did our feelings change?

How did we feel we were the same, or different?

MY RESPONSE: _____

_____

_____

_____

_____

_____

YOUR RESPONSE: _____

_____

_____

_____

_____

_____

What was the best thing about you?

MY RESPONSE: _____

_____

_____

_____

YOUR RESPONSE: _____

_____

_____

_____

Was there anything I wanted to change about you?

MY RESPONSE: _____

_____

_____

_____

YOUR RESPONSE: _____

_____

_____

_____

As we got to know each other, how did my feelings change?

MY RESPONSE: _____

_____

_____

_____

YOUR RESPONSE: _____

_____

_____

LOVE GROWS

Describe how you were feeling as our relationship grew more serious.

What did your friends have to say?

MY RESPONSE: _____

_____

_____

_____

_____

YOUR RESPONSE: _____

_____

_____

_____

When did you first think you might be falling in love?

MY RESPONSE: _____

_____

_____

_____

YOUR RESPONSE: _____

_____

_____

_____

Describe a memorable moment from around that time:

MY RESPONSE: _____

_____

_____

_____

YOUR RESPONSE: _____

_____

_____

_____

"I love you not only for what you are,
but for what I am when I am with you."

— *Elizabeth Barrett Browning*

PART THREE

Counting
The Ways

LOVER'S CHALLENGE

Pick just a few words to fill in the ultimate love list.

The one word I'd use to describe you:

MY RESPONSE: _____

YOUR RESPONSE: _____

Our relationship is like:

YOUR RESPONSE: _____

_____

MY RESPONSE: _____

_____

Some more words that describe you:

MY RESPONSE: _____

YOUR RESPONSE: _____

Your best qualities are:

MY RESPONSE: _____

_____

YOUR RESPONSE: _____

_____

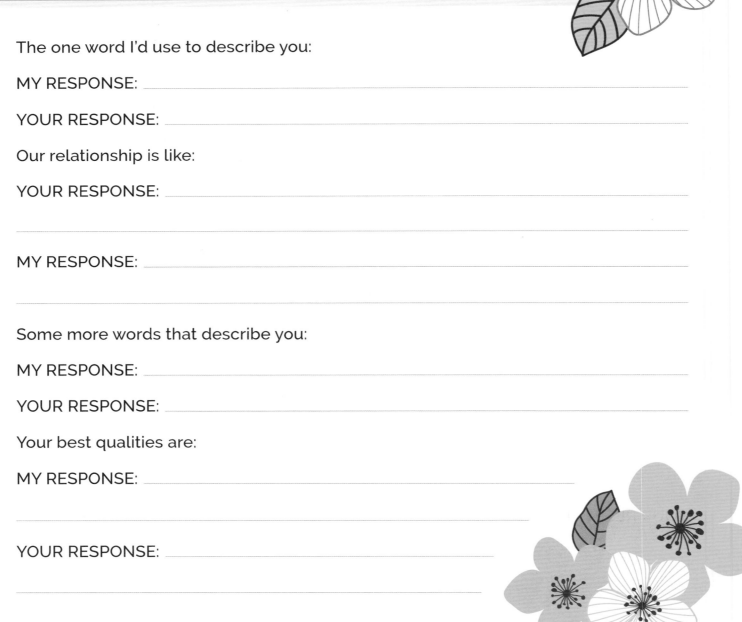

You're irresistible when you:

MY RESPONSE: _____

_____

YOUR RESPONSE: _____

_____

But I'm not so sure about it when you:

MY RESPONSE: _____

YOUR RESPONSE: _____

How you make me happy:

MY RESPONSE: _____

_____

YOUR RESPONSE: _____

_____

What I love when we're together:

MY RESPONSE: _____

_____

YOUR RESPONSE: _____

_____

What I miss when we are apart:

MY RESPONSE: _____

_____

YOUR RESPONSE: _____

_____

YOU'RE
THE BEST THING

You make me feel:

MY RESPONSE: _____

_____

_____

YOUR RESPONSE: _____

_____

_____

I couldn't live without your:

MY RESPONSE: _____

_____

_____

YOUR RESPONSE: _____

_____

_____

You give the best hugs. They make me:

MY RESPONSE: _____

_____

YOUR RESPONSE: _____

_____

Here's how I'd describe your smile:

MY RESPONSE: _____

_____

YOUR RESPONSE: _____

_____

The things nobody does better than you:

MY RESPONSE: _____

_____

YOUR RESPONSE: _____

_____

The top three reasons you're the best:

MY RESPONSE:

1. _____

_____

2. _____

_____

3. _____

_____

YOUR RESPONSE:

1. _____

_____

2. _____

_____

3. _____

_____

LAUGHTER AND LOVE

One of the times we laughed the hardest was:

MY RESPONSE: _____

_____

YOUR RESPONSE: _____

_____

Remember an event that sparked a running joke or ridiculous nickname that still makes us laugh to this day:

MY RESPONSE: _____

Running joke or nickname: _____

What happened: _____

_____

Your RESPONSE: _____

Running joke or nickname: _____

What happened: _____

_____

How would I describe the sound of your laugh?

MY RESPONSE: _____

_____

YOUR RESPONSE: _____

_____

What one word can you whisper to me, even in a serious moment, to crack me up?

MY RESPONSE: _____

YOUR RESPONSE: _____

Tell me a joke:

MY JOKE: _____

_____

_____

_____

_____

YOUR JOKE: _____

_____

_____

_____

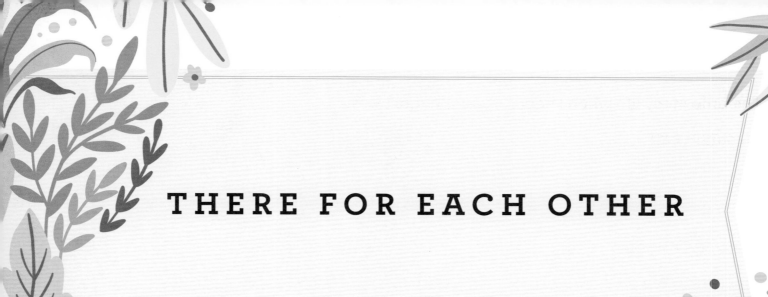

THERE FOR EACH OTHER

One of the most difficult times we've been through together was:

MY RESPONSE: _____

_____

_____

YOUR RESPONSE: _____

_____

_____

This was something I had to do alone, but I always wish you could have been there with me:

MY RESPONSE: _____

_____

_____

YOUR RESPONSE: _____

_____

_____

The time in my life when I needed you the most was:

MY RESPONSE: _____

_____

_____

YOUR RESPONSE: _____

_____

_____

And you were there for me by:

MY RESPONSE: _____

_____

YOUR RESPONSE: _____

_____

Here is what I want you to know about why I'll always have your back:

MY RESPONSE: _____

_____

_____

YOUR RESPONSE: _____

_____

_____

"Love recognizes no barriers."

— *Maya Angelou*

SECRETS AND (LITTLE) LIES

Shhh! This is a secret we kept between ourselves:

MY RESPONSE: _____

_____

_____

YOUR RESPONSE: _____

_____

_____

This is one time I totally covered for you. You owe me one!

MY RESPONSE: _____

_____

_____

YOUR RESPONSE: _____

_____

_____

I need to come clean. This is something I talked to family and friends about behind your back:

MY RESPONSE: _____

_____

YOUR RESPONSE: _____

_____

Did our secrets ever get us into trouble?

MY RESPONSE: _____

YOUR RESPONSE: _____

What were the repercussions?

MY RESPONSE: _____

_____

YOUR RESPONSE: _____

_____

Confession! What little white lies have I told you?

MY RESPONSE: _____

_____

YOUR RESPONSE: _____

_____

LOVER'S TIFFS

The biggest fight we've ever gotten into was...

Our biggest fight, how we got over it, and what we learned from it:

MY RESPONSE: _____

_____

_____

YOUR RESPONSE: _____

_____

_____

I know you're upset when you:

MY RESPONSE: _____

_____

_____

YOUR RESPONSE: _____

_____

_____

I try to help by:

MY RESPONSE: _____

_____

_____

YOUR RESPONSE: _____

_____

_____

What's your way of making up after a lover's tiff?

MY RESPONSE: _____

_____

_____

_____

YOUR RESPONSE: _____

_____

_____

_____

"It is a curious thought, but it is only when you see people looking ridiculous that you realize just how much you love them."

— *Agatha Christie*

THE THINGS WE DO
(AND SAY) FOR LOVE

Add a collection of memorable things we've said to each other, or done

for each other, or use the space for treasures and keepsakes from our

relationship. Both of you may add labels to explain the significance.

This is the perfect place to add a love letter, or two.

PART FOUR

Happy Together

LOVE STORY

The couple in a movie, book, or TV show that is most like us is:

MY RESPONSE: _____

_____

Because _____

_____

YOUR RESPONSE: _____

_____

Because _____

_____

If our story were a movie, it would be this genre:

MY RESPONSE: _____

Because _____

YOUR RESPONSE: _____

Because _____

_____

The actor who would play you would be:

MY RESPONSE: _____

Because _____

YOUR RESPONSE: _____

Because _____

_____

The actor who would play me would be:

MY RESPONSE: _____

Because _____

YOUR RESPONSE: _____

Because _____

_____

The movie title would be:

MY RESPONSE: _____

YOUR RESPONSE: _____

_____

Describe the ending:

MY RESPONSE: _____

_____

YOUR RESPONSE: _____

_____

_____

WE STAY IN TOUCH

How we connect. (Circle one for each row.)

HOW WE CONNECT:

(Circle one for each row)

BY TEXTING:	Almost nonstop	At least once a day to see how you're doing	Once in a while	I don't text
ON SOCIAL MEDIA:	All the time, about everything	I wouldn't know what you are up to without it	I look at your feed sometimes	I don't do social media
BY PHONE:	A few times a day	At least once a day	Now and then	Just text me!

Do we talk to each other enough, not enough, or too much?

MY RESPONSE: _____

_____

YOUR RESPONSE: _____

_____

Do we use any silly/special names for each other? How about secret signals?

MY RESPONSE: _____

YOUR RESPONSE: _____

_____

The topics we talk about most are:

MY RESPONSE: _____

YOUR RESPONSE: _____

The topics we like to avoid are:

MY RESPONSE: _____

YOUR RESPONSE: _____

The toughest conversation we've ever had was:

MY RESPONSE: _____

_____

_____

YOUR RESPONSE: _____

_____

_____

I'll never forget this phone call with you:

MY RESPONSE: _____

_____

_____

YOUR RESPONSE: _____

_____

_____

HANGING OUT

When we're together, we nearly always:

MY RESPONSE: _____

_____

YOUR RESPONSE: _____

_____

These are some of our favorite places to go:

MY RESPONSE: _____

_____

YOUR RESPONSE: _____

_____

Pets we've shared our love with:

MY RESPONSE: _____

_____

YOUR RESPONSE: _____

_____

Our idea of a perfect night together is:

MY RESPONSE: _____

_____

YOUR RESPONSE: _____

_____

Something fun we used to do that we haven't done in a while is:

MY RESPONSE: _____

_____

_____

YOUR RESPONSE: _____

_____

_____

The bravest thing we've tried together is:

MY RESPONSE: _____

_____

YOUR RESPONSE: _____

_____

But the best thing ever to do with you is:

MY RESPONSE: _____

_____

YOUR RESPONSE: _____

_____

FAVORITE THINGS

Color:

MY RESPONSE: _____   YOUR RESPONSE: _____

Time of day:

MY RESPONSE: _____   YOUR RESPONSE: _____

Time of year:

MY RESPONSE: _____   YOUR RESPONSE: _____

Holiday:

MY RESPONSE: _____   YOUR RESPONSE: _____

Books:

MY RESPONSE: _____   YOUR RESPONSE: _____

TV shows:

MY RESPONSE: _____   YOUR RESPONSE: _____

Movies:

MY RESPONSE: _____   YOUR RESPONSE: _____

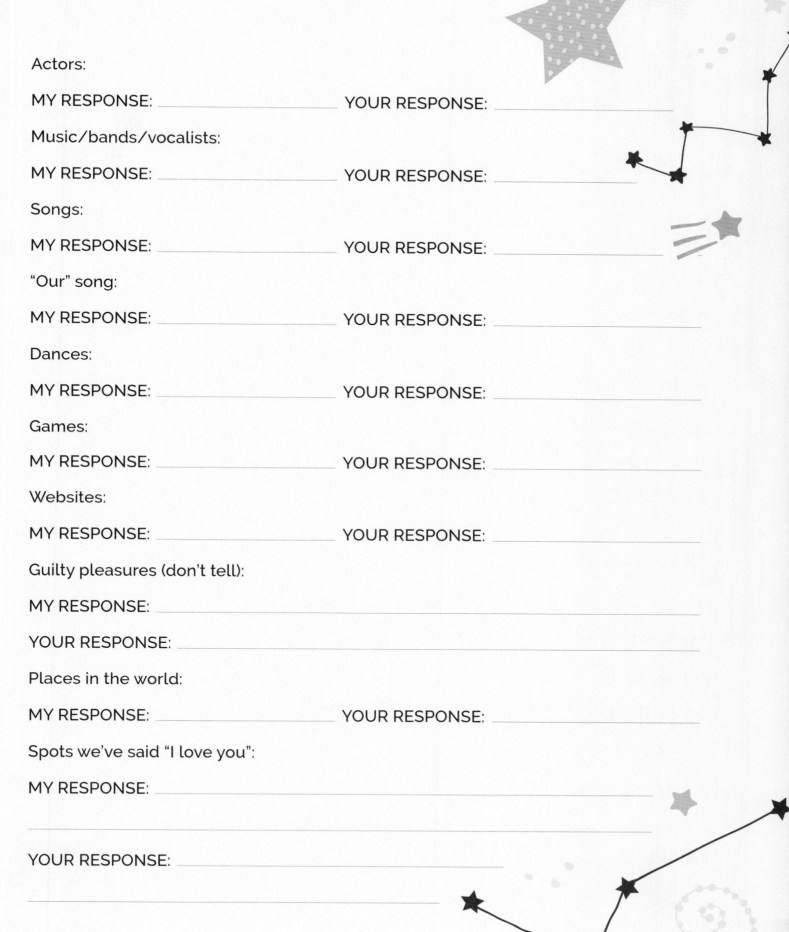

Actors:

MY RESPONSE: _____ YOUR RESPONSE: _____

Music/bands/vocalists:

MY RESPONSE: _____ YOUR RESPONSE: _____

Songs:

MY RESPONSE: _____ YOUR RESPONSE: _____

"Our" song:

MY RESPONSE: _____ YOUR RESPONSE: _____

Dances:

MY RESPONSE: _____ YOUR RESPONSE: _____

Games:

MY RESPONSE: _____ YOUR RESPONSE: _____

Websites:

MY RESPONSE: _____ YOUR RESPONSE: _____

Guilty pleasures (don't tell):

MY RESPONSE: _____

YOUR RESPONSE: _____

Places in the world:

MY RESPONSE: _____ YOUR RESPONSE: _____

Spots we've said "I love you":

MY RESPONSE: _____

_____

YOUR RESPONSE: _____

_____

FOOD OF LOVE

My top three foods:

MY RESPONSE: _____

YOUR RESPONSE: _____

I love it, but I can't believe you don't like to eat:

MY RESPONSE: _____

YOUR RESPONSE: _____

Our fave restaurants:

MY RESPONSE: _____

YOUR RESPONSE: _____

Takeout night! Hit the couch with:

MY RESPONSE: _____

YOUR RESPONSE: _____

The most memorable meal we've ever had:

MY RESPONSE: _____

YOUR RESPONSE: _____

Surprise! I'm cooking tonight. Here's the recipe for something you'll love:

MY RESPONSE: _____

Ingredients: _____

_____

_____

Instructions: _____

_____

_____

_____

_____

YOUR RESPONSE: _____

Ingredients: _____

_____

_____

_____

_____

Instructions: _____

_____

_____

_____

If you were a dessert or a candy bar, you'd be:

MY RESPONSE: _____

YOUR RESPONSE: _____

My love potion for you:

MY RESPONSE: _____

YOUR RESPONSE: _____

LOVE IN STYLE

I would describe your style as:

MY RESPONSE: _____

_____

YOUR RESPONSE: _____

_____

My favorite outfit you wear is:

MY RESPONSE: _____

YOUR RESPONSE: _____

I remember how amazing you looked dressed up in this for a special occasion:

MY RESPONSE: _____

_____

YOUR RESPONSE: _____

_____

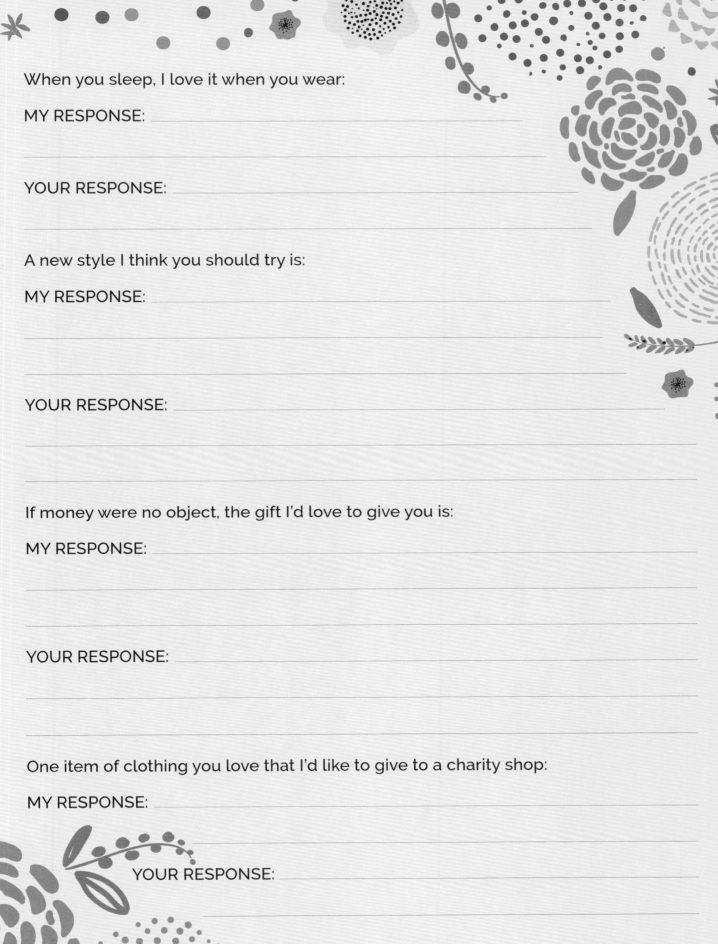

When you sleep, I love it when you wear:

MY RESPONSE: _____

_____

YOUR RESPONSE: _____

_____

A new style I think you should try is:

MY RESPONSE: _____

_____

_____

YOUR RESPONSE: _____

_____

_____

If money were no object, the gift I'd love to give you is:

MY RESPONSE: _____

_____

_____

YOUR RESPONSE: _____

_____

_____

One item of clothing you love that I'd like to give to a charity shop:

MY RESPONSE: _____

YOUR RESPONSE: _____

_____

PROUD MOMENTS

Describe a favorite holiday moment we've shared:

MY RESPONSE: _____

_____

_____

YOUR RESPONSE: _____

_____

_____

How about a brilliant birthday?

MY RESPONSE: _____

_____

YOUR RESPONSE: _____

_____

Every day is special with you. I was really proud of you when you accomplished:

MY RESPONSE: _____

_____

YOUR RESPONSE: _____

_____

Another time I was really happy for you was when you:

MY RESPONSE: _____

_____

Because _____

_____

_____

YOUR RESPONSE: _____

_____

Because _____

_____

_____

You make me proud ever day because:

MY RESPONSE: _____

_____

_____

YOUR RESPONSE: _____

_____

_____

I WANT TO THANK YOU

Thank you for teaching me:

MY RESPONSE: _____

_____

_____

YOUR RESPONSE: _____

_____

_____

Thank you for opening my mind about:

MY RESPONSE: _____

_____

_____

YOUR RESPONSE: _____

_____

Thank you for talking me out of:

MY RESPONSE: _____

_____

_____

_____

YOUR RESPONSE: _____

_____

_____

_____

_____

Thank you for saving the day when:

MY RESPONSE: _____

_____

_____

_____

YOUR RESPONSE: _____

_____

_____

_____

FOR THE FOLLOWING PAGES, TALK TO EACH OTHER, BRAINSTORM TOGETHER, AND WRITE DOWN YOUR IDEAS

You've made a whole book full of memories so far. Think about what you can do together to make even more, and make your mark as a couple in love.

COUPLE'S BUCKET LIST

WORKING TOGETHER FOR OTHERS

A project we've talked about doing together is _____

_____

_____

This feels important or exciting to us because _____

_____

_____

Here's what we need to do to make this project a reality: _____

_____

_____

_____

A cause we care about together is _____

_____

_____

_____

Here are a few ideas for how we can get involved: _____

_____

_____

_____

How can we "pay it forward" as a couple? _____

_____

_____

_____

_____

MAKING TRADITIONS

What are our milestone dates as a couple? _____

_____

_____

What can we do together to celebrate them? _____

_____

_____

Who will we share our new traditions with? _____

_____

_____

Set a goal for making a new tradition: _____

_____

_____

PEOPLE WE LOVE

Who are the people who have shaped our lives as a couple—parents, grandparents, siblings, relatives, neighbors, friends, coworkers—and what are some ideas for things we can do together to thank or celebrate them? Spread the love!

Person: _____

What we could do: _____

_____

_____

Person: _____

What we could do: _____

_____

_____

Person: _____

What we could do: _____

_____

_____

Person: _____

What we could do: _____

_____

_____

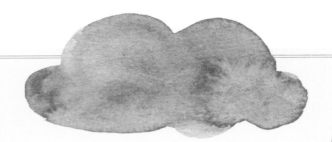

ONE PERFECT DAY

We've had countless amazing days, but what would be a perfect day with each other? What would we do, where would we go, what would we eat, and what memories could we create, from sunrise to set?

MY RESPONSE: _____

_____

_____

_____

_____

YOUR RESPONSE: _____

_____

_____

_____

_____

THE LOVE CHALLENGE

We only live once. Let's challenge each other to do something that might be a little out of our comfort zones or ambitious, but that could be life-changing.

I dare you to _____

_____

_____

YOUR RESPONSE: _____

_____

_____

Challenge accepted? Yes / No way *(Circle one)*

You dare me to _____

_____

_____

MY RESPONSE: _____

_____

_____

Challenge accepted? Yes / No way *(Circle one)*

Double down. We dare ourselves to do this together: _____

_____

_____

_____

LOOKING BACK

*Page back through the responses you've written in this book
before answering these questions.*

What is the most surprising thing you've learned about your partner in these pages?

MY RESPONSE: _____

_____

_____

YOUR RESPONSE: _____

_____

_____

Is there something your partner wrote about here that surprised you? If so, how did

that make you feel?

MY RESPONSE: _____

_____

_____

YOUR RESPONSE: _____

_____

_____

Is there something new that you learned about how you relate to your partner?

MY RESPONSE: _____

_____

_____

_____

YOUR RESPONSE: _____

_____

_____

_____

How did reading these pages make you feel?

MY RESPONSE: _____

_____

_____

_____

YOUR RESPONSE: _____

_____

_____

_____

PART FIVE

Let's Make a Forever

MY HOPES FOR YOU

My hopes for you are...

MY RESPONSE: _____

_____

_____

_____

_____

_____

_____

_____

_____

_____

_____

_____

YOUR RESPONSE: _____

_____

_____

_____

_____

_____

_____

_____

_____

_____

_____

_____

_____

_____

_____

_____

MY HOPES FOR US

My hopes for us are...

MY RESPONSE: _____

_____

_____

_____

_____

_____

_____

_____

_____

_____

_____

YOUR RESPONSE: _____

_____

_____

_____

_____

_____

_____

_____

_____

_____

_____

_____

_____

_____

_____

_____

_____

TRULY, MADLY, DEEPLY

Don't ever doubt it. These are all the ways and reasons I love you:

MY RESPONSE: _____

_____

_____

YOUR RESPONSE: _____

_____

_____

Some of the little things that mean the most to us:

MY RESPONSE: _____

_____

_____

YOUR RESPONSE: _____

_____

_____

The most fun we've ever had without trying:

MY RESPONSE: _____

_____

_____

YOUR RESPONSE: _____

_____

_____

It's hard to choose the sweetest moment, but it might just be:

MY RESPONSE: _____

_____

_____

_____

_____

_____

YOUR RESPONSE: _____

_____

_____

_____

_____

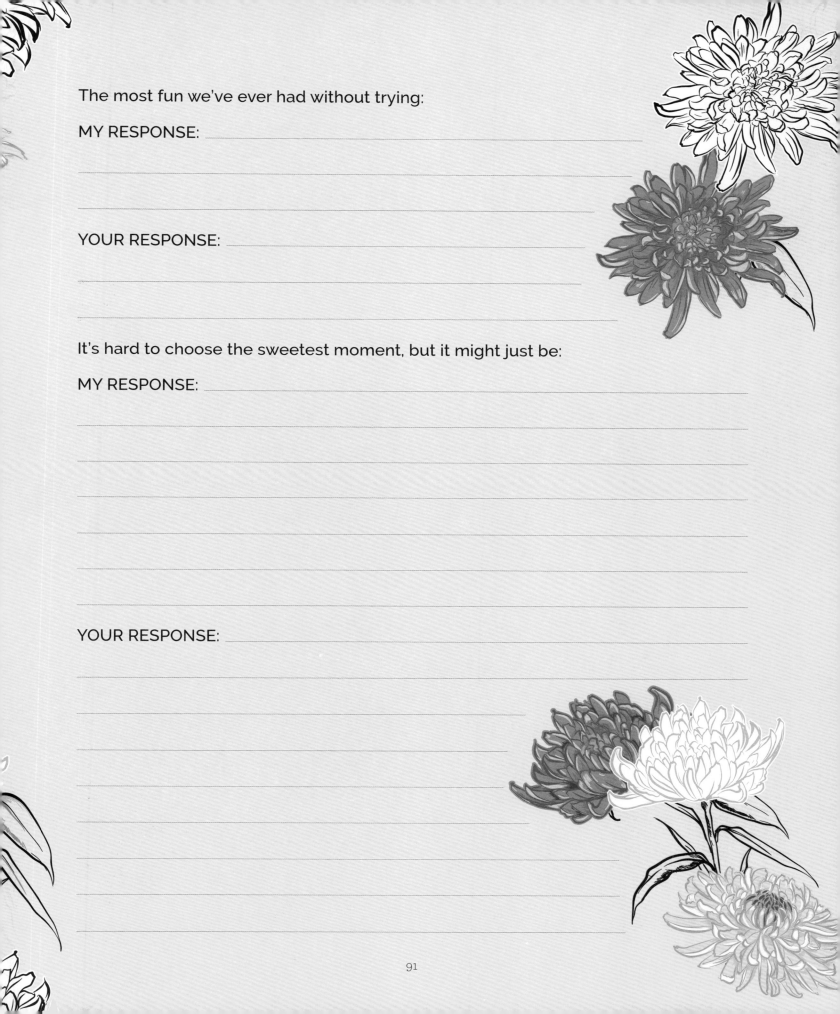

EVERLASTING

How can we keep a love like ours alive? Think about the ways we'll make our relationship grow and bloom.

MY RESPONSE: _____

_____

_____

YOUR RESPONSE: _____

_____

_____

Describe a challenge that we met together, and how:

MY RESPONSE: _____

_____

_____

YOUR RESPONSE: _____

_____

_____

Love's never sorry, but I am sorry about:

MY RESPONSE: _____

_____

_____

_____

YOUR RESPONSE: _____

_____

_____

_____

If we promised each other one thing, it would be:

MY RESPONSE: _____

_____

_____

_____

_____

YOUR RESPONSE: _____

_____

_____

_____

_____

MESSAGES OF LOVE

If you wanted to share one thing our love story has taught or shown you with future generations, what would it be? Write your message in a bottle here.

MY MESSAGE: _____

_____

_____

_____

_____

_____

_____

_____

_____

_____

_____